Communicating to Win
In Life, Love, and Business

Communicating to Win
In Life, Love, and Business!

By Bob Paff

Communicating to Win: In Life, Love, and Business

Copyright by Communicating to Win, LLC

The information contained in *Communicating to Win: In Life, Love, and Business* is meant to serve as a comprehensive collection of time-tested and proven strategies that the author of this book has applied. Summaries, strategies, tips, and advice are only recommendations by the author, and reading this book does not guarantee that one's results will exactly mirror the author's results. The author of *Communicating to Win: In Life, Love, and Business* has made all reasonable efforts to provide current and accurate information for the readers. The author will not be held liable for any unintentional errors or omissions that may be found.

No part of this publication shall be reproduced, transmitted, or resold in whole or in part in any form, without the prior written consent of the author. All trademarks and registered trademarks appearing in *Communicating to Win: In Life, Love, and Business* are the property of the author.

All copyrights belong to their respective owners. The word mark "Communicating to Win" is a registered trademark owned by Communicating to Win, LLC. This book and its contents are the copyright of Communicating to Win, LLC.

ISBN-10: 1505615984

ISBN-13: 978-1505615982

Dedication

This book is dedicated to my children: Zach, Taylor, Olivia, Carter, Logan, and Isabel Paff. It is out of my sincere love and devotion to all of you that I was able to put one foot in front of the other on days where it looked like I didn't have the energy to do so! I think the ability to effectively communicate is the crown jewel of life. I hope that, in some way, I have given you this gift, whether it comes in the form of learning from my mistakes or benefiting from my insight.

Finally, and ironically, I dedicate this book to all of you that have disappointed me, failed me, or let me down in some way—or have been let down by me. For, without these life-altering experiences, this book would have never been possible. You gave me windows into your souls and characters that will forever change the landscape of the world I live in. Through your pain, suffering, and life experiences, I was able to carve out the platform for *Communicating to Win*! A platform that if consistently applied will forever change the lives of those who embrace it.

Table of Contents

A Message from the Author..i

Acknowledgments..v

Introduction Communicating to Win...1

SECTION I: LIFE PHILOSOPHIES

Chapter 1 Humble Beginnings...7

Chapter 2 Defining Success 15

Chapter 3 Strength in Failure 21

Chapter 4 Embracing Adversity 31

Chapter 5 Letting Go 35

Chapter 6 Faith in Belief 39

Chapter 7 Keeping Your Head on Straight.....................................43

Chapter 8 Taking Responsibility 47

Chapter 9 Work-Life Balance 51

SECTION II: EMPOWERMENT

Chapter 10 The Business of You 57

Chapter 11 Begin with the End in Mind...61

Chapter 12 Who's on Your Team? 65

Chapter 13 Impressions..69

Chapter 14 Getting Out There 75

Chapter 15 Getting What You Want 79

Chapter 16 Putting It All Together 85

Chapter Lessons to Empower You!...89

More from Bob Paff and Communicating to Win!.......................91

A Message from the Author

Why this book, and why now? While it may sound self-indulgent to say, I always felt, from the time I was a small boy, that I was destined to lead a life of significance. Maybe it was the altar boy in me; maybe it was the result of being from a broken home.

Whatever the reason, I, like most of you, have lived a life of highs and lows, triumphs and tragedies.

But along this bumpy road, I have learned a thing or two I feel compelled to share with you. As Fr. Pete, my parish priest calls it, my ministry.

Ever feel so driven to do something that you couldn't stop even if you wanted to?

The book and my message within it are a culmination of my wealth of life experiences, observations I made both up close and from afar. While I would not wish these life experiences on anyone, I would also not trade them in for a more serene, sheltered life.

Life is for the living. As Eckhart Toule tells us in *The Power of Now*: "Life is difficult." Life is not so much about going through the daily motions; for me, it's more about what you do with those experiences, which will shape and transform you if you allow them to come in!

For some, for many, the pain of self-discovery is too great a price to pay for an uncertain future. What happens if I go down this road, only to experience more pain and disappointment?

We've all heard the saying that God only gives you as much as you can handle. That load is different for all of us. Believe me, I have had my surrender moments, times I felt I could not possibly persist in following my dream or, as I now say, giving into the little doubtful voices in my head that told me I couldn't do it. What always kept me going was the love and support of those family members and friends around me who believed in my message and understood the need to share it and make a contribution to the world.

As a single father of six children, my sole responsibility is to give them the tools needed to "surthrive" in this world. Yes, while *Merriam-Webster* does not recognize the word *surthrive*, it is perfectly suited to what I mean. Don't merely survive, thrive, using all the amazing energy and talent you have, all the blessings God gave you to live a full, rich, and rewarding life.

While this book is not religious in nature, I must admit and embrace my spiritual roots. Regardless of your religious affiliation, I do believe we all need faith—faith in ourselves, faith in a higher being guiding us to where we are supposed to be. A constant source of unconditional love and support when the big, bad, cruel world comes calling, and it will!

As a society and as a world, fundamentally, we are poor communicators at best. No one really teaches us how to communicate. We are left, in large part, to our own devices to "figure it out" on our own. Why? Because the problem is systemic, as no one taught our parents and, in turn, they didn't teach us. So, how can we teach our children or friends?

After all, we do teach people how to treat us by what we expect and accept from them, and yet, that causes us great anxiety and frustration in so many areas of our life. We are bound and handcuffed to the ugly monsters of embarrassment and rejection, forever living in fear of speaking our minds by asking for what we want and what we need.

What happens to these feelings if they are not expressed? Do they go away? No, they manifest and grow to the point where they wreak havoc on our lives and the lives of those around us. This book, the message, and the lifestyle proposed are answers to those age-old problems and inefficiencies in the way we communicate.

The ramifications, if properly applied, could change the world. The message crosses all political, religious, and socioeconomic boundaries. We have to change the way we do things, my friends.

You may have heard that the definition of insanity is doing the same thing over and over again but expecting a different result. *You* are the only one who can make that change happen.

Communicating to Win begins with you. It describes how to gain the ability to get clear within yourself on what it is that you really want from your life first, so that it can be expressed to others when the need arises.

We tend to complicate what it is that we truly want, when the truth is that we were already were born with that clarity but have lost touch with it. A child points at what he wants, smiles when loved, and cries when sad.

I cannot think of one example when I have listened to my gut and it led me wrong, but I have countless examples of the opposite.

Often, listening to oneself is the most difficult first step, for we let the opinions of others rattle inside our heads directing our actions or, more precisely, our inactions.

What follows in this book are my learned life lessons, experienced over the many pivotal moments in my life that many of us have in common. I share them openly to help you become a better and more effective communicator in all areas of your life.

May you gain the insight, courage, forgiveness, strength, and permission to allow yourself to be the best you there is by embracing the very thing that has set me free—Communicating to Win!

Thank you for joining me on my life journey; it will be great traveling with you!

—Bob Paff

Acknowledgments

While my message has been woven over a tapestry of over fifty years of trials and tribulations, triumphs and tragedies, this book would not be possible without the hard work, dedication, and loyalty of friends and associates.

I met marketing strategist and consultant Luke Harlan a few years ago when this journey began. Luke and I started down a different path, but all roads kept leading to *Communicating to Win* as a life-fulfilling platform.

We collaborated, drafted, and redrafted many a message or story until arriving at this final result. No relationship is without its bumps and bruises and we have had ours. Staying the course with a dedication to the core message is just one of the many commitments we share. This first in a series would not be possible without Luke's insight, intelligence, quick wit, and ability to make it happen on such short notice. He gained the ability to start and end many of my sentences. Thanks, Luke!

I encourage you to connect with Luke and learn more about him at www.lukeharlan.com. He has been an invaluable resource.

Also, I would be remiss not to mention just a few folks who may not even be aware of the contributions they made to this collaborative process, for no one writes and creates alone. My thanks to Dave Foertsch, Aliza Rosen, Ashley Andersen, Reghan Swenson, Amy Emmons Blackstock, Susan Purifoy, Eli Eisenberg,

Rob Woodward, Ginny VonBussenius, Diane Marsiglia, Gisele Soto and Betsy Royal. And I will never forget a casting director friend telling me I was too big for Baltimore and needed to move to New York, or Amanda Manown, the riding instructor I had who suggested I belonged to the world, which stuck in my head as a source of constant pride and encouragement to see the project through.

No doubt, there are many others who touched me in some way along this journey and I am deeply and perpetually grateful.

Finally, I need to acknowledge my faith in God and the strength I receive daily from my church community at the Cathedral Mary Our Queen in Baltimore. It is a community that has sustained me in more ways than they will ever know.

Introduction

Communicating to Win

The single biggest problem in communication is the illusion that it has taken place.

— attributed to George Bernard Shaw

Some years ago, my primary vocation was as the president of my own insurance company, helping physicians in all stages of their professional growth to protect their families and grow their assets.

While not a sexy business, it was none the less practical, beneficial, and often lucrative. However, after twenty years of being in this profession, there were voices inside me that kept getting louder. Ones that said there was more that I could be doing...should be doing.

I've heard them before and slowly began to realize they only went away or were temporarily muted after speaking at various insurance industry events a few times a year.

While I always felt energized and renewed afterward, I made no real connection to why that was and would simply roll back into the day to day of my company operations.

One day, in a moment of clarity it hit me that the type of speaking that made me feel energized was not about insurance! It was about helping empower, motivate, and inspire the other carriers, agents, and brokers to be better for their clients and themselves. My purpose now revealed, I started building my new public-speaking business.

I remember sitting in my office one day figuring out what this new business should be called, when I had an epiphany. That voice in my head I was finally listening to screamed out...

"Communicating to Win!"

It was perfect. We all communicate on a daily basis. Whether you're communicating with your wife, your children, your business partner, your in-laws, or your neighbors...on a daily basis, we all have to communicate.

We also all want to win and it's a relative term, just like success is. Yet, I haven't met anybody, whether they are preschoolers or CEOs, who doesn't want to win. You just need to define what that means for you, but I think everybody is in agreement. I haven't met anybody yet who says, "I want to lose."

Communicating to Win covers all areas of our lives: socioeconomic, religious, political, business, and personal, as everybody has to communicate and everybody wants to win.

However, many are not doing this well or at all. Unfortunately, many of us model our behavior on that of others. Yet, just like with us, no one is helping them understand how to put together the pieces in order to get what they want. They simply do not have the tools to do this.

Instead, we retreat, not advance when faced with the opportunity to succeed in various areas of our life. We do this for many reasons, but much of it comes down to our base psychological wiring.

As humans, our instincts go back to the fight-or-flight response. While none of us are currently staring down the jaws of a *T. rex*, asking for a promotion from your boss, soliciting for new clients, speaking with your kids about sex, or even bringing up that special intimate fantasy you may have to your partner is no less daunting.

Often times, we freeze up and talk ourselves out of the very actions that we absolutely need to take in order to get what we want out of life. We do this because our decisions are hardwired into two main objectives.

Those are to either seek pleasure or avoid pain...and when you focus on avoiding pain, it often leads to overwhelming and paralyzing fears.

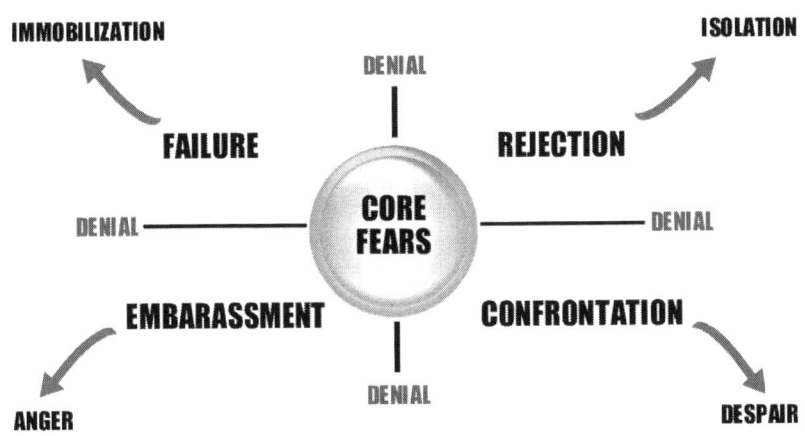

Fear of failure, fear of rejection, fear of embarrassment, and *fear of confrontation.* We let those fears immobilize us and we retreat back into our corners and convince ourselves that those perceived fears are a worse consequence than the actual pleasure we would receive if we had moved forward.

This is denial, and not just denying through rationalization but denying the possibility of a better life, career, and relationships!

The worst part of this is that we all know this to be true. We can feel it in our gut and the less we do and less we accept the fears, the more isolated, angry, and in despair we become.

However, there is a solution. There is a way to take control of these fears, and it starts with learning how to effectively communicate what you want first and foremost with yourself.

Everyone has a breaking point, but it should never come to that. We are not created to see how much we can take before making the decision to change the course of our lives for the better.

This is a decision that is ours to make, and while we cannot control much of the outside world, we can control ourselves. What and how we think. What we say and how we say it. And this is the heart and soul of *Communicating to Win!*

So, be true to yourself and be open to those insights, revelations, and shifts that will make the difference in your life.

SECTION I

LIFE PHILOSOPHIES

Chapter 1

Humble Beginnings

Whatever you are, be a good one.

— attributed to Abraham Lincoln

Abraham Lincoln has inspired me in so many ways. With his courage, conviction, insight and indomitable spirit. Where would we be as a society, as a nation, without this simple man from Illinois?

One of my favorite of his quotes, "Whatever you are, be a good one," reminds me of a story I tell often about my son Taylor coming home from work after his first day of a new job at a local restaurant.

Taylor walked through the door complaining, "Dad, I can't work there; people are rude, demanding, and difficult. Everyone is so hard to please."

My son, blessed by God with enormous gifts of love, patience, and kindness, was about to get one of the best lessons of his life, compliments of Abraham Lincoln!

I looked Taylor in the eye and, without an ounce of hesitation, told him that working in a restaurant would be one of the best learning experiences of his life. The ability and the skill of being able to manage people at their best and worst would prepare him for a lifetime of success and failure.

I told him to remember that little if any of the behavior his patrons exhibited had anything to do with him. They probably woke up that morning in a bad mood; had a fight with their spouse; or went to a job that they hate with a boss, partner, or employees they don't want to be around.

I explained that his job, as is the job of anyone in the service business, is to show his customers a great experience. It's not the one hundred dollars they are paying for the seafood dinner; it's the one hundred dollars they are paying for the "dining experience," and that must be the focus of his accommodations.

Finally, in the great words of Lincoln, I reminded my son that he would not always be a waiter but that the life experiences gained from such a wonderful job would last him a lifetime and help him to deal with the unpleasantness that others, both strangers and loved ones, sometimes throw at us!

While I did not have the luxury of a dad who was any way involved in my life, having left our family when I was ten, I think God blessed me with the spirit of Lincoln in allowing me to have, at a very tender age, a solid work ethic and a commitment to a job well done.

I was also bestowed with a conviction that told me that if I did one thing well, I deserved a chance at the next opportunity that came along. A sense that I had earned the right to ask!

If only we could predict where life would take us, then we could plan better. The late author Stephen Covey said in *The Seven Habits of Highly Effective People*, "Begin with the end in mind," which is a difficult philosophy for most of us to follow and even more so for a twelve-year-old working his first job.

In my case, the job was setting up bowling pins in the basement of a church for three dollars a night. There were only three lanes, so the opening was hard to come by. It meant one of the three boys had to be injured, move away, or get fired for a spot to open up! So, when I got the call, I was ready.

Growing up in the inner city with parents who were employed as a legal secretary and factory worker, I didn't balk at three dollars a night. I was delighted to have the job and there was no question I would work my butt off to keep it.

I remember that job like it was yesterday, and looking back I gave it no consideration that one good deed would present another opportunity. I simply felt a compelling desire to work hard and leave a good impression.

Whether my work ethic came from nature or nurture, I can't be sure. I can only point to my brother who delivered newspapers and was always the first one to be done with his route. Unfortunately, it turned out that he was dumping his papers down the sewer to finish early in order to get paid for as little work as possible, as opposed to signing his name to it and doing a solid day's work. Instant gratification was his order of the day!

Those early days instilled in me a sense that more lay ahead for me beyond status, upbringing, or where I lived.

Years later, I marveled over that I was living in one of Baltimore's historic neighborhoods that as a young boy, I knew only as a neighborhood where "rich people" lived.

Now, rich is a relative term as you age, as we often define it relative to our own standards and how others perceive us. Whether it's rich in material possessions, money, status, and fame; or rich in the simple pleasures of life such as treating others as we ourselves want to be treated; or simply even rich in the satisfaction of completing a day's work worthy of signing our name to it.

However, as Robert Kennedy said, "To whom much is given, much is expected." This same twelve-year-old boy, feeling destined for greatness in whatever form life had in store for him, would go on to share the stage with the likes of Rudy Giuliani—...another man of humble roots who has left his mark on the work and led us through 9/11, one of the greatest tragedies of our lifetime.

There is a joke in politics that every politician grew up in a log cabin that they built themselves. It is so funny that we spend our lives trying to better ourselves, and in some ways to escape the roots of our childhood, only to return years later and celebrate them as our humble beginnings.

How many of us have forgotten those roots, the very foundation of our character, our work ethic, and our legacy?

As a society, we have lost our personal background and are often adrift in a sea of immediate gratification thinking that "stuff," and not who we are, defines us. No longer are we concerned about producing work that is so good that we would "sign our name to it."

This is the very fabric we must repair if we are to regain and maintain our place in the world and raise a generation of hardworking children rich in character and integrity, and full of commitment to themselves, their families, and others.

I cherish those roots. For me, there was no log cabin but a very modest home with two parents for my first ten years, until my dad left us. We all need an anchor, some reservoir of strength to tap into when the times get tough as they will.

My character and work ethic, humbly rooted in that house on Duncan Street, allows me as a grown man to walk the line from barroom to boardroom.

Often when I do public speaking, I am judged by my outward appearance, the second I walk on stage or enter a room. What is it about gray hair and a navy-blue suit that makes everyone think you're wealthy?

Often, I begin my talks by playing a game where I ask members of the audience to look at me come up with two or three words to describe what they perceive me to be.

My one rule: be kind in your assessment! It's only after hearing the predictable words like *rich, successful, powerful,* and the like that I divulge my past.

Eyes pop out and jaws hit the floor when I tell everyone about the inner city Baltimore neighborhood where I was born, went to school, and spent the formative years of my life.

I have very fond memories of taking two buses across town to get to school from the time I was in first grade. And of my brother and I staying home by ourselves until our parents arrived home from work, usually around 5:30 p.m.

We didn't know the term *latchkey kids* until we ourselves had children. Times were either different or parents and children much more naïve; I choose to think the former, not the latter.

So, what does it say to my judgmental audience when I disclose that the neighborhood I grew up in now requires a pistol and an armored vest to walk through in broad daylight?

It sends an immediate message that I was not born on third base pretending I hit the triple. It tells them I know their plight, feel their pain, and can genuinely connect. Most important, it allows their filters and blinders to come off so the message can sink in.

Those humble roots have grounded me and made me into the person I am today, personally and professionally.

While many do seek to run and hide from their past, the true value is in looking ahead to see how far you have grown but always keeping one eye planted on where you started.

This allows you to be the authentic you.

Notes:

Chapter 2

Defining Success

Always bear in mind that your own resolution to succeed is more important than any other.

— attributed to Abraham Lincoln

Are you good at what you do? Do you promote yourself? Would you sign your name to your work?

We all define success differently, as success is a totally subjective achievement. For some, it may be a big fancy car or the address of the family home being on the right street. For others still, it is defined by life balance or a contribution to society and community.

However, the one key thing we all need to do more of is to "take ownership" of what success means to us and then learn, believe, and practice what it takes to achieve the goals that will bring about that success.

Additionally, you need to be honest with yourself about exactly what those goals are. For those goals will serve as your motivation, and unless that motivation is strong and compelling enough, you will not see them through. By owning our success and also our failures, we become a model of future behavior for those closest to us.

With a world that bombards us with minutia every second of every day, it is easy to become distracted and lose sight of what really matters. It is also challenging to stay focused on your strengths and passion.

From the time we are young, we are taught to "work on our weaknesses." What I say, now and always, is to play to your strengths and delegate your weaknesses. Those things we tend not to be good at will always lag behind our passion. In the areas that need work your progress toward efficiency will only improve slightly, while your fulfillment of your passion and strengths will take you places beyond your wildest dreams!

Herein lies one of life's biggest deterrents to success and dreaming big.

Not everyone, sad to say, wants you to have all the success you are capable of having. Why, you may ask. This fact of life speaks to my philosophy that just like we purge our wardrobe, we need to purge those who keep us from living what our intended purpose is.

Throughout my years, I have seen support turn into rejection and ridicule when one friend becomes more successful than another or when one neighbor goes out and buys the fanciest car on the market.

Why can't we be genuinely happy for others?

You may think it is because of the big, green monster called jealousy. However, it goes deeper than that. You see, in our eyes, if we are not living up to the expectation that we have for ourselves and others have for us, seeing the material success of others is like a constant reminder of what we are not, of what we have not achieved.

Sadly, we process another's success as our failure. However, you cannot and should not allow someone else's accomplishments to define you or stifle your success, in whatever way you measure it.

You need to be true to yourself and wake up every day knowing *you* and *you alone* define and measure your own success as it applies to you. That no one has the same commitment or passion to your goals as you. Only you can make that happen!

Whether it's "Keeping up with the Joneses" or "What would the neighbors say?" the bottom line is that the clearer you get with what you want and why you want it and the less apologies you make, the more free you will be to obtain that thing.

Small towns and small cities tend to be full of local celebrities, the proverbial big fish in the small pond. It's nice to walk into any establishment and have people recognize and acknowledge you.

For some, it's enough to be set far away from the crowd but still get the warm, cozy feeling they are loved and adored by the masses.

After running my own financial services firm for over twenty-three years and after my second marriage ended, I ventured out into what ironically was my first true love—the media.

I suppose you could argue it's like riding a bike: you never forget!

Moving head on and full speed into acting, modeling, and voice-over work, almost by accident, I met with some immediate success. But others who have toiled and practiced their craft or their art for many more years than me did not; do not appreciate the perceived rapid success of anyone, not just me.

Is anyone truly an overnight success? I have lived over fifty years and been branded with the battle scars to prove that it's not that simple. Under the pretense of "giving you advice," others in their own way try to bring you down.

How does he do that when I have been working at this for twenty years? Why did she get those "lucky" breaks after I sacrificed so much? You and I have heard it all, if not directly then certainly secondhand.

Do we create our own luck? In other words, is our success, or lack of, predetermined?

It is incredibly difficult, arguably impossible for most, to stand in the face of adversity and rejection and march onto what they feel is the gold at the end of the rainbow.

We quit too soon; we sacrifice our drive and ambition for those of others; we convince ourselves that it will be okay to enter the golden years of our lives with only regret and bitterness.

The noted psychologist Erik Erikson covers this in his theory that there are eight stages of man when he talks about generativity versus despair, looking back and coming to terms with what did and did not work, dreams given up on, and passion never ignited.

What is it that you hold yourself accountable to that measures your success, in whatever form that may be, so that you know if you are on the right path and giving yourself the opportunity to achieve it?

Notes:

Chapter 3

Strength in Failure

Every adversity, every failure, every heartache carries with it the seed of an equal or greater benefit.

— attributed to Napoleon Hill

Fear of failure is a primary force in our lives that prevents many from ever trying and thus ever succeeding. However, failure is really just another opportunity for us to get it right. When you look at it as a measuring device and not a personal barometer of your potential, then you'll welcome the lessons it provides and gain strength in yourself for moving one step closer to achievement.

Failure is a building block to learn from and is simply the word we use to describe the undesired outcome of an event or action. There are countless examples of people that have literally reshaped our lives, history, technology, science, imagination, and commerce that failed time and time again before becoming who we know them for today.

Abraham Lincoln lost his job and was defeated in six elections prior to ever being president. Albert Einstein's teachers said he would not amount to much. Michael Jordan was cut from his high school basketball team.

The Beatles were rejected from a prominent recording studio and told they had "no future in show business." Walt Disney was fired from a newspaper for "lacking imagination" and having "no original ideas."

Harry Potter author J. K. Rowling was rejected a dozen times and told to "get a day job" and that there was "no money in children's books." Oprah Winfrey was demoted from being an anchor and told she "wasn't fit for television."

Steve Jobs, at thirty, was kicked out of the very company he had founded. Thomas Edison failed at over one thousand other inventions before bringing the world the electric lightbulb, the phonograph, and the motion picture camera.

And then there were Thomas Jefferson, Henry Ford, and Milton Hershey, who all went through bankruptcies, among dozens of other political and financial leaders.

Can you even imagine the world in which we live if any one of these people had given up or quit at the first, or even twentieth, sign of failure?

It would have been so easy for any one of those folks to give up at any point. However, they would not tell you that they've had a lifetime of failure nor assign personal defeat to failure.

They intentionally chose to believe failure is what it is. A teacher to learn from and move forward…and so can you!

The Chinese proverb "There is great opportunity in pain" is one of my all-time favorites. It gives us another opportunity to come to the plate, to use the sports metaphors so many identify with.

So, if this is the case, why do so many quit so soon? It's a known fact that in most sales positions you have to hear the word no seven times before you get the yes you're looking for. And yet, so many quit too soon, after the second or third no, and in some cases after the first negative response. Whatever happened to "If at first you don't succeed, try and try again"?

Can it not be said that the no response is merely a rudimentary way of asking for more clarification? Why is it that we always assume finality or go to the ultimate negative? It is a critical and fundamental breakdown of our own internal communication or "self-talk" that leads us to our own "self-defeat."

Remember, how you react to the outcome of your efforts is completely up to you. You can own it or allow it to own you. It's your choice and always has been.

There is tremendous strength in failure. The key is to accept it for what it is and take it as a learning opportunity to do better next time.

Just as I'm not certain that anything truly "bad" happens, I'm also not convinced that we look at failure the right way. It was Thomas Edison who said that failure is just another opportunity to do something better. I think Edison was a very wise man!

The tragedy in the mistakes or errors of failure is not learning from them. All that pain, all that suffering, for what? Can you look back at the greatest "failures" in your life and point to lessons learned from each of them?

Are there any failures you would not have wanted to miss out on? Have any of your failures defined who you are and how you look at the world?

Tragedy and failure can be two of the most life-changing experiences you will ever have. But for this to happen, your sense of awareness must be fully opened up in order to allow the growth that only failure can bring to seep into your life.

The single most-defining failure in my life was the end of both my marriages. They will always be my greatest regret and greatest textbook.

My convictions in marriage, fidelity, honor, and commitment were firmly rooted the day I discovered my father was having an affair with my mother's best friend. I was ten years old, and, whether unknowingly or selfishly, my dad made me an accomplice to his deception. Young but not stupid, his excessive and obsessive attention to another woman struck me as odd if not flat-out wrong.

My mom had a schedule like clockwork, and every Wednesday when she would play Bingo with her sister Mary, my dad would head over to her best friend's house while her husband was working the night shift at a local meatpacking plant.

My dad, keeping his own clock, would come back fifteen minutes before my mom's arrival home and tell me, if she asked, that he had been home all night.

I wondered why my dad would ask me to say that when it simply wasn't true! From that day forward, he turned me into Dick Tracy, Kid Detective. I watched his every move, his every encounter with this woman.

While ten-year-old Catholic-school boys know nothing about sex, the voices in my head and the knot in my stomach told me something was terribly wrong.

That summer, Dad's house of deception came crashing down when we went away for a week in Wildwood, New Jersey, on a vacation with the other woman and her son! Riddled with her own pain at the soon-to-be end of her troubled marriage, my mom turned to me for comfort and answers.

While way too young to have any interest in knowing and seeing the worst of adult human behavior, I was a dedicated and loving son to my mother and would have done anything to "rescue" her from that pain.

Little did I realize that would be the birth of my "rescue fantasies," but that's another story altogether! I held the cards to whether my dad would come back and the influence or exposure he had to our family.

My only sibling, dealing with his own pain as his super hero dad had just taken a monumental fall to earth! His life would go on to be riddled with heartache and abusive behavior until he died a month shy of his fifty-fifth birthday from liver cancer.

Thinking I had survived with just a few battle scars in place, I married in 1984, when I was in my twenties. My new wife and I had been friends for years; she was like the sister I had never had.

My once-wife's own dad, himself unfaithful, had wreaked his own havoc on her family, having a woman and house on the side for some ten years before finally divorcing her mom. I was convinced we were on solid ground, having witnessed firsthand the devastation caused by morally corrupt fathers.

In 1998, after four children and fourteen years of marriage, the woman who had been like a sister to me before we married had her own very public, very humiliating affair!

Two families, seven children in total, worlds turned upside down. Within a year of filing for divorce, I was a single dad with four children at thirty-eight years old.

My second marriage had all the warning signs not to go there. I recall a friend describing my soon-to-be wife as having too many "fatal flaws." Her failed first marriage, her natural father's departure when she was young, and the list went on.

Anyone having lived through this much pain and denial surely had scars on top of scars. My fatal flaw was in assuming she would do the work necessary to turn great pain into opportunity and would break the cycle once and for all, at least for our own children.

Some habits die hard, if they ever die at all. I had not buried my habit of always trying to be the rescuer engrained in me as a child helping my own mother. Wasn't it attributed to Churchill who said, "Those who fail to learn from history are doomed to repeat it"?

When that marriage ended in 2010, and arguably much earlier, there was little surprise. While she rapidly moved on into another relationship, for fear of being alone among other things, I threw myself into my work and devoted my time and attention to our two young children, ages nine and soon to be eight.

The next two years were spent in therapy and in church trying to figure out how it all fell apart, or if, in fact, it was ever together. The details are not significant to this book, but the rise out of great pain is.

Reaching a benchmark of middle age as this marriage came apart, I finally came to terms with the notion that we cannot fix others, nor can we love them more than they love themselves.

Immersing myself in this pain, I found myself spending more time on others' needs than on my own.

I prayed and I had the loving support of a few loyal and trusted friends, but I never, ever gave up the hope that I would come out smarter, stronger, and better equipped than I had gone in.

I would never wish this pain of an unfulfilling, lonely marriage that was hanging on by a thread on anyone else, and as a result of it I felt even more compelled to share my lessons to help others avoid the same fate.

Without truly knowing what you want, which only comes from really asking the hard questions, we tend to keep returning to the familiar and repeating the same mistakes.

This is why divorces rates are significantly higher for second and third marriages and why it is even more critical to break this pattern.

The real work comes in fostering an air of safe communication by creating a forum where you can be free of any chance of embarrassment, rejection, or ridicule—marriage in which the ability and luxury of being vulnerable is celebrated and embraced every day.

Those failures changed me forever, but they were given to me by a loving and merciful God who would only point me in the direction of freedom, knowledge, and peace. The blessing is that I listened. My story is not unique. It's told countless times across the globe by people who are innocent, sheltered, or in denial every day.

The beauty, your gift and opportunity, comes in turning all of that into something positive for you, your children, and those around you.

There is great opportunity in pain, and for that I'm forever grateful!

Where might have you "failed," and did you embrace the lesson it taught you in order to move on?

Notes:

Chapter 4

Embracing Adversity

You don't know what you don't know.

— Bob Paff

Failure, as previously discussed, can be a good thing. However, in order to not repeat past mistakes, you need to take it a step further and uncover the truth behind the failure.

This can be a difficult but very freeing process at the same time. Too many times, we are afraid to admit our shortcomings—that maybe we're not the best employee, boss, father, husband, lover, or friend. Yet, might you also not consider that acknowledgment a good thing since it tells you that that this is an issue and you can now address it?

Aside from extreme tragedies that defy rhyme or reason and can sometimes destroy or even define us, I am not convinced that there is not generally anything truly "bad" that happens to us. Just like failure, it's how you interpret and learn from it.

I'm thinking of a book I once read called *When Bad Things Happen to Good People* by Rabbi Harold Kushner. In most all of the tragedies we encounter, there are always some life-changing experiences that surface. Our challenge is to embrace the adversity and go deep to find the true meaning behind the event.

One of my favorite talks is called, "Embrace Your Adversity." I like to call the challenging moments the wake-up moments of life.

There was a three-year period where I saw no less than the end of a marriage, personal misfortune in business, and the death of my only sibling, all to then be faced with the prospect of redefining myself.

Some of these hardships are never faced over the course of one's lifetime, yet I had the pleasure of them being delivered all at once, most without warning.

This adversity in my own life has caused me to reach out, not only for explanations, but also for sources of guidance and emotional support. We all have those mornings when we would just love to pull the covers back over our heads, hit the alarm clock, and call it a day, never getting out of bed.

While that refuge does provide a temporary respite, it's never the answer. Some days, the only thing to get you motivated is the knowledge that others are counting on you for their very own direction.

What I have learned through the process of embracing all this adversity is to listen to the little voices in my head. It's fascinating to me that as the older I get, the louder the voices become. Is it because I'm losing my hearing, or is my conviction that much more profound now that I've aged a bit?

While I fall short of suggesting that you actively seek adversity, I do fully support the notion that you should embrace and uncover it. There truly is gold in "them there hills" and to the one who can persevere the effort will have been well worth it.

One caution I would make: Sometimes the other side of the adversity is total transformation. Perhaps you have been living or leading a life for others, doing things on automatic pilot, because that's the way you have always done it. Once the blinders come off, you are left standing on your own, and the opportunity is before you and you alone to take that leap of faith.

Don't go quietly into that dark night. Grab a shovel, run like hell, and get ready for revolutionary change. You deserve it!

Notes:

Chapter 5

Letting Go

Some people believe holding on and hanging in there are signs of great strength. However, there are times when it takes much more strength to know when to let go and then do it.

— attributed to Anne Landers

The basic principle continuing from embracing your adversity is learning how to be honest with yourself. When adopting the *Communicating to Win* philosophy, you may need to do a gut check every morning when you wake up as you define that which will move you closer to your goals.

How am I feeling today? What am I anxious about? What am I struggling with? How do I tell Mary this? How do I tell Tom that?

How do I go into the office and communicate what I need? This isn't working for me—what do I do about it?

When doing this exercise to identify what it is that may be holding you back today, what you find may surprise you. While Sigmund Freud says that our personalities were formed by the time we were five, it is actually the collective impact of our past experiences that defines us.

For the most part, we do not consciously associate any of our decisions with the interactions we had with siblings, parents, schoolteachers, or the kids on the playground, as we tend to believe we are operating in the now.

However, whenever you take a new job or begin dating someone, your *baggage* comes with you. You're bringing everything that has happened in your life, as it is really the formation of who you are, something that we don't even think about.

Sometimes the *reality* that we have outgrown a relationship or a situation is so palpable that it causes us pain. We're irritable and short tempered—perhaps some physical signs of the wear and tear this anxiety has caused us.

But often, we hang on for too long, afraid of what letting go might present us with. While the pain of staying is real, it's not quite as bad as the fear of the unknown.

Maybe your mother has referred to this as the "Devil you know for the devil you don't." It takes an especially strong person to walk away from any negative situation, personal or professional.

Over time, we may even come to see ourselves as the culprit: if only I could do this or that, give others what they want from me, my life would be more complete.

I am reminded of a lunch date I had with a divorced female friend who had recently broken up with a guy after three years. She began to describe the reasons as a conflict between children from previous marriages, lifestyle issues, and financial concerns, among other subjects. She further went on to claim that she had transformed him from a modest, rural guy, content in his world, to a "beautiful" man and to proclaim all that she had done for him.

I asked her if she wanted my sugarcoated version or my direct and unfiltered opinion of what happened. After all, I love it when women pretend to know exactly how we men think as we profess to know their thoughts.

I told her to move on and let it go. The relationship had given them three years of pleasure but it had run its course. There was no passion left in the tank, only frustration and despair. Why not this and why not that!

My friend had remade her guy into what she wanted him to be, what suited her. In the process, this gentleman lost himself. He was now just a reflection of her; uncomfortable in the fine linen clothes she bought him. I told my friend that if she were to bend and break to make this work, she would compromise her very soul and still never be happy. Neither party was right or wrong. It was not necessary to place any blame, so what would be the point?

I suggest to everyone at this phase of their job, their relationship, their friendship, that when being together becomes more work than joy, go ahead and listen to the little voice saying it's time to let go!

Embrace the experiences you shared and move on, knowing that it helped bring you to where you are now. Without this experience, you would not be the person you are today. Don't fear the uncertain future or assume that you will have a life of loneliness.

Where is it written that being alone means being lonely? For some of us, sadly this day never comes. We can never find the strength to cut the strings and move on. For others still, including myself, it comes late in life, but better late than never.

All the experiences leading up to this moment have made you ready to be fully accepting and appreciative of the life you were meant to lead.

Stop living in the shadows of others and step into your own ray of sunshine! You have a choice. You can let it go. I chose to let it go. I chose to share it.

What's holding you back?

Chapter 6

Faith in Belief

If you must doubt, doubt your doubts...and never your beliefs.

— *Anonymous*

My faith has gotten me through, I think, probably...not *some of* the worst times, but *the worst* times in my life. The highlights being two failed marriages, the roller coaster ride of business, confronting past demons, and daily struggles with my six children, for starters. Yes, six kids! It is safe to say that whatever the challenge has been, I've been grounded in my faith.

Now this is not a proclamation that everyone needs to adopt a religion as his or her belief system, only that a belief as well as a support system of any kind is helpful when navigating the rigors of life.

For me, I grew up as an altar boy going to Catholic school. Not unlike any other kid who was dragged to church by his or her parents, I can look back and know that it was there that my seed of spiritually was planted and took root.

Instilling such a belief system is how I have imparted to my own kids, while they might have been twisting and turning in the pew out of boredom, that at some point in their life they will be thankful to have this foundation to go back to.

I tell my kids that you're never alone, that there's a higher being, and for those who believe in God, God's always with you. The key is in the belief and if it's not God, Buddha, Yahweh, Allah, or whichever entity, then what?

What belief do you have that can help you sustain your drive, your energy, your conviction, and be the backbone of your spirit? Whatever it is, no one truly succeeds alone. We all need to fall back and lean on that which is greater than ourselves for comfort and strength.

So, my faith has gotten me through a lot of times when I was ready to say, "You know what? It's not worth it. I can't do this anymore. I give up. I quit."

Whatever you want to say, I always come back to faith and say, "Okay, I can do it one more day." So you break it down and take one day at a time. But I think my faith has been absolutely critical to my survival as well as my success.

There are times we all need to lay our burdens down. Regardless of belief, try closing the door and speaking out loud about the subject you need the most help with. You may be surprised by not only how you feel expressing that out loud but also the clarity it will often bring in helping to solve your own problems or turning to those who can.

"Getting it out" is incredibly therapeutic, liberating, and necessary.

Find your source of strength and support and know that asking for help is not a sign of weakness!

Notes:

Chapter 7

Keeping Your Head on Straight

If you think you can do a thing or think you can't do a thing, you're right.

— attributed to Henry Ford

I would say that we all internally have a—let's use the word *spark* or *seed of success*—which is good news! However, we must acknowledge that there are external forces that can promote it, fertilize it, or even allow it to burn out. Forces that we ultimately end up letting into our decision-making process and belief systems.

The people in our lives, including our parents, siblings, colleagues, neighbors, friends, and classmates, can play such a huge role. All of them, when allowed, can influence how we think about ourselves and ultimately what actions we do or do not take.

Additionally, the environment itself can have a significant impact and immediate influence on us. News and media outlets breed fear by reporting all of the world's injustices daily. I believe the way we put it in the industry I was part of many, many years ago was, "If it bleeds, it leads," referring to which stories to choose to make the news.

If we only allow ourselves to be exposed to these influences routinely, then they will naturally breed anxiety, fear, and rejection. This puts us in an emotionally disadvantaged state from which to operate.

If Freud thinks that the majority of our personality is formed by the time we are just five years old, it is the interaction with our parents and siblings from the early days of our lives that is the basis on which our personalities are formed.

We teach others, from a very young age, how to treat us, what we will and will not tolerate. Even if we are unaware, we carry that behavior on into our adolescence and adulthood. In her wonderful book on parenting, *Strong Fathers, Strong Daughters: 10 Things Every Father Should Know*, Dr. Meg Meeker talks about the impact a father's love has on his daughter. This book, or the companion book for mothers and sons, should be given out in every maternity ward once the words, "It's a girl!" are uttered.

I cried like a baby when I myself first learned this for the first time while watching an off-Broadway play in New York. I felt like I had failed my daughter Olivia, now into her twenties.

Incredibly sad and incredibly frustrating is the fact that our unsuspecting life and business partners are usually never given this insight into our past. How frequently does this leave us on the road to disaster with our companions, with no chance in hell for success?

I used to say of a former business partner that I didn't like him. What I didn't realize until he left was really *how much*!

It is only when they are gone and we are not caught up in the discomfort of these people on a daily basis that are we able to be honest with ourselves.

If we were to receive a "life resume" from a potential business partner that disclosed that he had a father married at least four times and a mother riddled with alcoholism, we might have a choice as to whether or not to associate with this person.

When things go awry on the back end, you're left putting the pieces together to make sense of what looks like the unimaginable. Sitting alone in a half-empty office after a former business partner cleaned me out while I was on Christmas vacation, I never felt so alive and at peace.

Odd, you say? Not really. If you live by the theory and deep and abiding faith that everything happens for a reason, it simply becomes one more step toward a life or life ministry you were meant to lead.

There really is something to the notion of getting the eight-hundred-pound gorilla off your back! Life is way too short to spend it surrounded by people who secretly mock you, are envious of you, or for whom you conjure up some painful memory or reminder of everything they are not. In fairness, it must also be torturous as hell for them, too!

Ultimately, only we can be accountable for our actions and decisions. My friend, Fred Furney, who grew up with a love of cooking and wanted to be a chef was constantly beaten down by parents who insisted he "get a real job."

The sad truth is that his divorced parents had been carrying around their own bag of shit for years, sprinkling it on whomever and whatever they could to lighten their own load. Hopefully, we figure it out, which sadly few do.

Ultimately, it is your choice to only allow in those people and messages that you want to define you. I prefer to surround and enrich myself with like-minded, positive people as well as what they convey.

Be aware, be focused, and be in the moment!

Chapter 8

Taking Responsibility

You must take personal responsibility. You cannot change the circumstances, the seasons, or the wind, but you can change yourself.

— attributed to Jim Rohn

Too often, we view taking responsibility as simply doing what our clients, family, or friends expect of us professionally or personally while forgetting to first take responsibility for ourselves and how we manage our own affairs.

However, for me one of the greatest and most liberating moments was when I realized that these external responsibilities, while necessary, were truly secondary to the responsibility I had to myself first.

Simply put, that revelation is, how can you take care of others if you do not take of yourself first? This is not a proclamation or encouragement of selfishness but rather a self-evaluation to make sure what you truly want out of life is being addressed and protected.

For example, how many times do we say yes when what we really mean is no? We do things to please other people all the time, we do things for recognition, and we do things for acceptance, based on what's expected of us, not what we want to do.

Whether at work or in our personal lives, we are often asked to do something that either we can't do, would love to do but don't have the time, don't have the resources or skills to do, or simply don't have interest in doing, somehow we say yes. Why?

For many, it's the *fear of rejection, fear of embarrassment*, or *fear of abandonment* that actually goes against our internal gut barometer of what's right and wrong for us.

We all have an innate sense of what we should and shouldn't be doing. But, too often, we talk ourselves out of that sense at our own expense because of these "fears," which can set a pattern for our entire lives.

My pattern began back when I was ten years old and rescued my mother from her marriage to my father after discovering his affair. He left and then swore he had changed, so my mother then begged me to let him come back into the family. I said no, but she wore me down until eventually I gave in.

This first lesson of saying yes instead of no carried on throughout my life, in my other relationships, my marriages, and my work. I had not set the expectation for myself within myself. Inevitably, the damage caused by trying to please others or avoid confrontation significantly outweighed my perceived fears of what would happen if I said no.

So, without considering yourself to be crazy, you need to have a conversation with yourself about what your true priorities in life are. What is it that you truly want? Again, this goes back to defining your own success and taking ownership of it.

Part of this process is also distinguishing between things that are negotiable and things that are nonnegotiable on your priority list. Within any relationship, there needs to be give and take. However, being too flexible, or conceding that which was nonnegotiable, will only hurt you in the future.

The takeaway here is to first clearly communicate to yourself those expectations that you will later communicate with others.

There is a world of difference between *giving of* yourself for the sake of others and *giving up* yourself for the sake of others. The latter should never be asked of you.

Define and defend your priorities and rules of how you want to live your authentic life!

Notes:

Chapter 9

Work-Life Balance

There's no such thing as work-life balance. There are work-life choices, and you make them and they have consequences.

— attributed to Jack Welch

We all struggle with how to balance our time when it comes to work, family, and life. However, often it is actually our own perception of each that overcomplicates it all.

We tend to want to compartmentalize and separate who we are into different roles and responsibilities given our surroundings. Yet this may be shutting off the better parts of you.

While we all have our many roles in life as the boss, the employee, the parent, or the friend, we first and foremost are people. We take all of those things with us, consciously or not, into each environment.

We are setting ourselves up for failure if we do not recognize and accept that there is overlap in who we are for ourselves and who we are for others. This goes beyond carving out or prioritizing the actual time we spend within each environment to address how we spend that time.

The mom that fights to get the kids out of the house and to school on time only to arrive to work a little late will definitely bring that frustration with her and may be short with her counterparts. Just as the CEO who comes home at night still in work mode may bark orders to his family.

These things are not good or bad per se; they are the reality of our lives and just are. You need to recognize and be aware of them so you can communicate to those around you that they are not accountable or responsible for your actions, reactions, or behavior.

You then need to recognize that you may need a transition period or time to decompress from one surrounding or environment before you go to the next. It's okay to ask for a minute to do this.

Remember, it is difficult and often damaging to shut off or compartmentalize one area of life completely in favor of another, as it will end up creeping back in and often at the most inopportune time.

You may find yourself snapping at people and it may not have anything to do with what's going on then and there. It is the manifestation of that which occurred a couple of days ago.

What do you think is happening to that energy? Where do you think that energy's going? Do you think it being dissipated? No. You're taking it to the little league field. You're taking it to Starbucks. You're taking it to the office, to the bedroom, and to church.

Creating balance in your life is not as much about carving out the time as it is about recognizing the overlap, accepting it, and communicating it to yourself and others.

How much easier would it be on those in your life if you could say, "Allow me a few minutes to decompress and I'll join you in a moment"?

We all have bad days or bad things happen to us. However, you have a choice of how you express them to others and to yourself.

Remember that our actions have a very real and powerful ripple effect on others that unfairly rolls downhill.

Your baggage is yours to be dealt with by communicating effectively within yourself or back to the source. It is not to be passed down to burden others with unless you are constructively asking for help.

Be aware of what you are letting spill into your next environment.

Notes:

SECTION II

EMPOWERMENT

Chapter 10

The Business of You

You must be the change you want to see in the world.

— *attributed to Gandhi*

Being the business of you is the topic of one of my favorite talks that I gave, which came together by accident while speaking to a group of business owners and entrepreneurs, only to discover midway through that many in the room had been homeless.

I was there standing in front of a bunch of people all looking at me like deer in headlights when I realized I quickly needed to adapt my talk in midstream. Even for seasoned speakers, this can be quite the challenge.

How do you go from talking about corporate empowerment to talking to people who are struggling with the basic forms of survival—people whom the day before were sleeping in the park?

Fortunately those voices came to me and I said, "Well, if you're not in business, you need to treat yourself like a business." Then it hit me what were the core similarities between this group and students I had previously spoken to.

I love speaking to students. I've had graduate students and medical students at a lot of my talks and it's very interesting to observe them—their body language, their speech patterns, and where they sit in the room.

Usually the students sitting in the back, they're the ones not really paying attention; they're the ones who say—I will invariably ask people to get up and say maybe a little bit about themselves—"I'm just a student."

As a society, we tend to define ourselves and allow others to define us by our current occupation or situation and not by who we are and what we can become. This is why you should treat yourself as "Me, Inc." You are a business. You are the business of you. You are the product.

So if you're as student or you're a homeless person or you're whatever it is, wake up every day with a purpose. Wake up every day with a plan.

It might be sitting down the night before and deciding what you are going to do the next day. Am I going to make ten phone calls to try to find a job? Am I going to go visit a professor or my advisor because I'm struggling in this particular subject and thinking about changing majors?

Whatever you do, whoever you are, you are a business, and that Me, Inc. talk and that philosophy applies—again, it goes back to the *Communicating to Win* concept—to everybody. It absolutely applies to everybody to treat yourself as a business through every stage of your life!

Exercise the control you do have over your decisions, and the actions you take!

Notes:

Chapter 11

Begin with the End in Mind

The key is not to prioritize what's on your schedule but to schedule your priorities.

— attributed to Steven Covey

Whether it's business or personal, how can we "get there" if we don't know where "there" is? It's like trying to get to any new travel destination without your GPS or some form of direction.

When you get out of bed every morning, how do you start your day? You, of course, have your regular morning routine and then it's off to or into the office, with many working remotely these days.

But where are you going, and how are you getting there? Will you wake up at sixty-four and say, "I'm retiring next year, better get started on that game plan for life after sixty-five"? While my comments seem like simple commonsense, how many of us can answer all these questions by affirming that we have no course set out for our lives?

Why is it that we go through life on autopilot, dodging the proverbial bullets life throws at us every single day without a clue as to how to safeguard ourselves, our families, and our associates against them?

Would you bake a cake, build a house, or buy a suit or groceries without first knowing what to look for, what you want, and what you need? And yet we muddle through life-altering, earth-shattering, course-changing decisions every day.

We send our children to school, or our sales force and administrative teams out into the field without any sense of direction or intended long-term goals. We live for and in the moment.

How much more effective would you be if you broke down your goals into daily, weekly, monthly, and yearly increments? How much more focused, productive, happy, and grounded (not to mention less anxious) would your associates and family be if they not only knew what was expected of them but were armed with the specific tools to get them there?

There is no magic here. It is, like anything else, it's a process. Let me give that process so you can get started now, today, and tonight—tomorrow at the latest! Have that family or employee meeting to say, "Here's what we're doing, and this is your role."

Most people get their job laid out for them with clear-cut direction, expectations, and measures of accountability. Play to your strengths and delegate your weaknesses to someone on the team for whom they are strengths.

Your associates and family will be less anxious and more productive if they are not wasting time trying to read your mind.

Do it now and watch the results lower your blood pressure and increase your bottom line, whatever that might be!

Notes:

Chapter 12

Who's on Your Team?

You are the average of the five people you spend the most time with, including yourself.

— attributed to Jim Rohn

As life provides its share of ups and downs, we, as business owners, employees, parents, spouses, and friends, sometimes struggle during those down times and look for ways to raise ourselves back up.

However, too often we find ourselves surrounded by people who are merely comfortable with the status quo instead of ready to challenge us and not let us get off easy, or in a reverse scenario come to our rescue if need be.

This thought came to me when I was faced with tremendous hardship going through a bitter divorce, a dissolving business partnership, and all the fallout they both caused personally and professionally.

The thought that often crossed my mind during that dark time was, *Who's on my team?*

Who are my go-to people? Who, if I was absolutely down on my luck and eating dog food and living in a tent, could I go to without a doubt of that person being there for me? Who's going to tell me like it is, not what I want to hear?

Who are the folks you look up to, confide in, and perhaps want to be like? For many of us, it's not who we think; it may not even be the one you share your bed with, your most intimate dreams, and desires. I know for me those people weren't whom I thought. It was definitely not my soon to be ex-wife at the time or the distrusted business partner. They didn't have my back.

It's been said, rightly and understandably so, that to have a friend you have to be a friend. However, what does that mean? How do we define *friend*? What are the boundaries of friendship?

The hardships that many of us face in our lives really allow us to see who our friends are. While a painful test, for sure, the tragedies and failures of our lives will challenge and in some cases destroy what we once believed were indomitable friendships.

It can be all too close and all too uncomfortable for friends to even be around, let alone take a position. I remember being deeply hurt by the actions of a few when my marriages and business failed but uplifted and surprised at the support of others once they perceived I was sitting on the sidelines.

I ask you, I challenge you, I defy you, who do you celebrate, who do you champion and support, and what's the defining mark at which that support goes away?

Are we afraid to listen to our inner voice, to let our conscience guide us in the direction of what is right? Or is it easier to ride out the storm sitting high atop the fence, away from any flying shrapnel? It's always easier to do nothing, to have no voice, to appear to be impartial, or to suffer in silence because a spouse has been so vocal or critical about what happened.

Do we dare to venture out and celebrate someone wronged, ridiculed, or falsely accused? Isn't it much easier to remain silent since we have so many of our own issues, struggles, ghost in our closets?

Perhaps you'll find that celebrating others, supporting others, allows that flow to come right back to you. Haven't you ever heard the theory that one can have too much karma or pay it forward too far in advance or too much?

In the absence of the same old approach not working, does it make sense to listen to your heart, go with your gut?

If you lay your head on your pillow every night and count one or two solid people on your team, you are truly blessed in immeasurable ways.

We all have many, many acquaintances, but with everyone so busy and so challenged by their own problems, how many *true* friends do you have and to how many are you a *true* friend?

My suggestion here is not to go blindly and surround yourself with people who simply tell us what we want to here, quite the opposite to be exact.

It's incredibly difficult, impossible for many, to go under the microscope and have someone question their motivation, their way of thinking, their very behavior. Sometimes it takes the most painful, most tragic of life events to wake us up to this reality of who is and who is not on our team.

This is why it is so critical to your long-term success to have the right people on your side! Those you feel good when you're around. Those you walk away from feeling enriched and appreciated. Those you are you quite certain that no matter where the chips fell they would be there to help pick you up.

Inversely, do you provide this deep level of support for anyone? Are you the friend, spouse, associate, or neighbor you want those around you to be?

So, who's going to raise your game? Make you better? Who's on your team? I challenge you today! **Who will make a difference in your life or in your business tomorrow?**

Chapter 13

Impressions

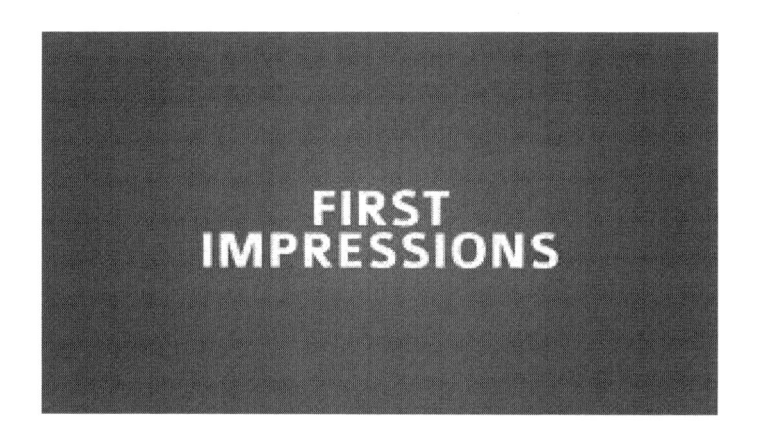

What you do speaks so loudly that I cannot hear what you say.

— attributed to Ralph Waldo Emerson

They say actions speak louder than words and how we are perceived from our first impression is lasting. However, impressions are usually so false, so misleading, and such a slippery slope for us to go down!

We look at each other and within the first fifteen seconds we have already placed what may be a permanent label upon the other person. We judge and misjudge people by the cars they drive, the clothes they wear, the friends they keep, and houses they live in.

Going back to the thought that we are the average of the five people we most surround ourselves with, we are indeed judged by the company we keep, not just the decisions we make.

Gray hair, trim and athletic at fifty-plus years old, navy suit—I am almost always mistaken for someone born into privilege. My most cherished talks have been given in homeless shelters to low-income individuals trying each and every day just to get by.

Why don't we dig deeper? Why don't we ask about someone we truly want to know? Why do we look at the gray hair, navy suit, and air of confidence and immediately shut down as though that person has nothing to offer or nothing constructive to say?

Whose responsibility is it anyway when others miss the mark and falsely mislabel us?

Is it ours for wanting to be perceived a certain way or theirs for not digging deep enough or asking the right questions? One of the many rewarding things I have had in my life is the ability to walk in the shoes of many people.

I often laugh at those running for office that claim to have been born in the log cabin they built themselves, only to forget who and what got them there once they are elected.

When those of great privilege, not necessarily great wealth, are asked to feel the pain of the average person, is that humanly possible unless you have had or shared a similar experience?

I think of former Speaker of the House Nancy Pelosi. Perhaps it's her Baltimore roots, but in many ways, I think she personifies what it's like to be out of touch. Now, be careful in drawing conclusions about my comment, as is our nature.

I am not saying anything negative or offensive about Mrs. Pelosi; it's just a matter of how you interpret what I said. Is it possible for a woman with such a strong political family history who went on to great wealth and political success to understand how someone sleeping on a storm grate really feels? Of course not.

How can politicians, while running for office and telling you they "work" for you, have any sense of the real world when they are escorted around in chauffeur-driven cars with security detail? When they are accorded the accolades and adulation we readily give our rock stars, athletes, and celebrities!

It's a disjointed, unfair, cruel world we live in and it gets more challenging and disenfranchising for so many every single day. The world cannot and will not pick you up unless you take the emboldened first step.

This reminds me of a verse from a song of one of my favorite singers. Adele has a great line in one of her songs that says, "Next time, I'll be my own savior." If you won't do it, no one will do it for you. Others might assist, for a while, but no one will *ever* carry the torch for your success, your message, like you will.

Just as it was attributed to Gandhi years ago, "Be the change you want to see in the world". You must be the voice and the force behind your own convictions, ready to accept the good and the not so good that comes with that.

Impression can be so misleading, by you and about you!

However, the common mistake people make when looking to start a business or personal relationship is trying to be something they are not.

As we discussed earlier, for fear of rejection they try to please the other party without consideration of the expectation they are setting and against their own favor.

We work too hard at things. We work too hard at making things work that either should not work or do not work.

Ultimately, being an authentic version of you versus being a cheap imitation of somebody else or something else will help you achieve and attract the right partners, clients, customers, and friends into your life.

When you think about your life and ask, "Do I have friends that like and support me?" the answer is of course you do. And why is that? Because you were being you. Business is no different. Be yourself. Be genuine.

Think about when you first meet people. We instinctively and often unconsciously size others up. We judge people within the first few seconds.

We look at a person and ask if he or she mirrors me in some way? Do I like what that person is wearing? Do I like how that person looks? Am I comfortable in this person's presence? Do I feel overshadowed by this person's presence?

However, we are equally conscious of the person sizing us up, and that is often when you start thinking of how he or she wants you to behave.

How does this person want me to sound or look? It's funny because if I'm speaking to somebody who is an English teacher, suddenly in my head I'm thinking about my grammar and imagining that this person is going to be correcting it.

You need to be authentic. You need to be yourself. You need to embrace who you are, warts and all. Otherwise, the foundation of that relationship is one sided and ultimately deceptive and destructive to both parties.

Notes:

Chapter 14

Getting Out There

> Fears are stories we tell ourselves

You cannot build a reputation on what you are going to do.

— *attributed to Henry Ford*

The great immobilizer of achievement or success in any area of our lives is fear. *Fear of failure, fear of rejection,* or *fear of embarrassment.*

These fears cause us to retreat instead of advance. We often tend to go into denial and make excuses rather than confront the fears. We may even isolate ourselves to avoid even being faced with them.

I've discussed how to take ownership of our lives, define our own success, treat ourselves like a business, embrace adversity, and let go of the past. Fear is baggage that we pack and carry all on our own.

Yet, you have a choice to let it go and move onward and upward.

We all have our comfort zones, for better or worse. They are our default ways of handling various situations. These, as we have discussed, may be rooted in and modeled from our upbringing. The good news is that you are not beholden to the past even if that past was only yesterday.

The only way to work toward what we truly want is to get out and break free of these zones, the barriers that are holding us back from enjoying the success, the joy, and the love that we receive from our personal and business relationships.

The only cure is to take action and this is where having faith and belief is so critical. Sometimes, the hardest decision to make is to put yourself out there, to be vulnerable.

The truth is that it is only in this perceived vulnerability and risk that there are rewards.

While at times it is better to rip the Band-Aid off completely, it usually should be done incrementally. You can set up small tasks and steps that reinforce themselves when completed and, as you work, you will gain momentum that edges you out of that comfort zone.

You absolutely need to get out there. "There," for you, could be dating again after a divorce or talking to your kids about death, drugs, or even sex. "There," for you, could be networking to find new business clients or a new career. Or going back to school after twenty years.

Whatever it is that will bring you happiness, love, peace of mind, or the success you want is waiting out there for you.

The reality is that it is not fear that is holding you back. It is you holding yourself back by hanging onto that fear. Oftentimes, it is irrational and built up to a level much worse than the loss from not trying could ever get to. It has always been your choice.

I can tell you from experience that there is only one thing worse than all the real or even perceived fears out there—regret! As you grow older, you'll find the only things you regret are the things you didn't do.

Regret comes in knowing that all the possibilities of what could have been were actually in your control. Do not deny yourself the opportunity to succeed—or even fail—because, as we have already seen, that failure in itself is merely a stepping-stone and a building block to your success.

It all starts by putting yourself out there.

So, what is it that you've been holding yourself back from doing?

Notes:

Chapter 15

Getting What You Want

You can't always get what you want, but if you try sometimes, you just might find, you get what you need!

— Lyrics attributed to the Rolling Stones

What I find ironic in adulthood is that we are so fearful at times of asking for what we want, when as children, from the moment of our birth, we had no hang-ups about communicating everything we desired. A lesson we should return to.

While in the last chapter we explored and identified the various fears we have or built up in ourselves that can paralyze us, this chapter is about how we can overcome them, which you can!

You see, we are born with only two natural fears: the fear of falling and the fear of loud noises. Everything is else is a learned behavior. So, unless your goal is to be a skydiver or work in an artillery range, this is great news. For, what can be learned can be unlearned or replaced with something much better!

Think about a person who you wanted to date or do business with but never asked. What is the worst thing that could have happened? They could have said no and you would have been no further back than when you started, because the answer to the unasked question is always no.

As famous hockey player, Wayne Gretzky, said, "You miss one hundred percent of the shots you don't take." There is nothing to lose and everything to gain.

What happens, however, when you do get involved and it's not all you thought it was going to be? How do you extract yourself from that relationship?

We often avoid the confrontation at the inevitable expense of the relationship rather than having an open, honest, candid conversation with somebody.

What is more surprising is that they could be feeling the same way you feel about a situation, but it's a matter of who's going to be the one that takes that step, initiate that conversation, and say, "This isn't working for me."

They say the truth shall set you free. How often after having those difficult conversations do we feel so much better and liberated? And every time, it's because we were carrying that baggage, that eight-hundred-pound gorilla on our backs, and suffering needlessly because of it.

Again, those ingrained fears of rejection, embarrassment, or confrontation rear their ugly heads. We look to please others over ourselves, which, again, is a disservice to both parties.

I have had relationships that have ended and maybe I've said to a person, "I can't give you what you want right now." And it's so empowering to, first of all, ask those people what they want.

Know that not everyone will be in the same place you are. When you ask and discover what someone really wants, you'll find out that it is not necessarily in line with what you can provide. You now have given that person the license and freedom to accept what you're saying and to live with that or not.

We, again, are afraid of the response we will get. However, it all comes back to the idea that you cannot change or make a decision based on what you don't know.

When you ask for a raise, what are you truly afraid of—just getting a no or learning the reason for the no? Are you underperforming? Wouldn't you rather address the issue than live with the symptoms? What if it simply turned out that your boss was waiting for you to take the initiative and demonstrate you have what it takes ask for what you want?

Communicating to Win is about being open and honest with yourself and asking for what you want so that you can clearly communicate that with others who you wish to share your life with, at home and in the office and everywhere in between.

Ask and you shall receive. The answer may not always be what you want to hear but it will be what you need to hear in order to take ownership of and be in the driver's seat of your own life.

Taking control is not about actually having control. That is unrealistic, as there are too many moving parts in our lives.

It is about recognizing what is in your power to control, starting with how you think and how you communicate with yourself.

SUMMARY

Notes:

Chapter 16

Putting It All Together

Never look back unless you are planning to go that way.

— attributed to Henry David Thoreau

Benjamin Franklin said it best when he coined the phrase "The only way out is through."

This book, this collection of thoughts, comments, and stories, has been a journey. A journey of fifty-plus years that I am still on and will never stop enjoying and learning from until I take my last breath!

It is a shame that we can never peek into the future to gain some sense of why we are on this journey and know that eventually, with a deep and abiding faith, things always seem to turn out. I'm firm in my belief and conviction that we are all "where we're supposed to be" and that life truly starts at the "end of your comfort zone." Why is it, then, that we go back to those set points even when we know how toxic and damaging they can be?

Why is it so hard for some to move beyond the heartbreak and pain of life's lessons and see the light at the end of the tunnel?

One day, my son Taylor looked at me and said, "Dad, I have to tell you something." Not a comment most parents look forward to hearing from their son. I held my breath, imagining this was a request for money or a confession that he had chosen an alternative lifestyle—either would have been acceptable!

I was *not* prepared for what he would say to me. He said, "Dad, I don't want your life." Blown away by the courage it took for him to say that and the profoundness in its intent, I paused, gathered my thoughts, and said, "Taylor, I don't know if I wanted my life, but I've made the most of it.

"However, if as your father, I have taught you any lessons and given you courage to make decisions and freely speak your mind, I have done my job, and for that I am grateful."

It's sad to me that we don't get a rulebook for how to live this life or to be parents, the world's most important job! We muddle through, trial and error, hopefully more trial than error, and hope that at the end of the day, the end of the journey, the pros have outweighed the cons. That we will have left a mark, an impression, valuable lessons, and perhaps even a legacy for our children and those following them.

There's no value in being the Monday-morning quarterback, or living a life of regret and despair. Yesterday is gone and tomorrow is promised to no one!

So, as I bring my first literary book to a close, what's the final message, what do I really want to say?

I hold several theories of life near and dear, all of which I would have never come to without the experiences that have taught and molded me.

None of which would ever be possible if I didn't learn to listen to myself through trial and error. To have those hard conversations in the mirror that freed me to pursue the person who I have become.

At the end of the day, others will judge you as they see you, through their own life filter, a filter riddled with their own successes and failures, heartbreaks and pain, rejection and embarrassments.

These are not yours to carry. Let it all go, my friends!

Live the life you were meant to live and that God has in store for you.

Is it not better to be an authentic version of yourself than an imitation of others?

Notes:

Chapter Lessons to Empower You!

- Your job is to be the best **you** that you can be!
- Be **true** to yourself.
- There is **value** in your past.
- Hold yourself accountable to your **dreams**!
- Embrace the lessons from your **failures**; they are a gift.
- Never quit; **transformation** awaits on the other side of adversity.
- **Opportunity** is a door. *You* must be the one to decide to walk through.
- Asking for help is a sign of **strength**.
- Be aware, be **focused**, and be in the moment.
- **Give** *of* yourself but never give *up* yourself!
- Never ask others to carry your **baggage**; only ask for their help in setting it down.
- Treat yourself like a **business**. You are the CEO of Me, Inc.!
- Mind reading is rarely **effective**. Say what you want.
- **Growth** requires having people in your life that challenge you to be a better you.
- Nothing **starts** until you put yourself out there.
- In order to receive, you must first **ask**.
- Be **authentic**, be genuine, be yourself.

Always Communicate to Win!!!

More from Bob Paff and Communicating to Win!

Keynote Speaking

Communications expert Bob Paff and his empowering message can be brought into your business, organization, or association with his signature *Communicating to Win* keynote presentation.

Visit BobPaff.com for presentation and booking details.

Connect with Bob Paff on Social Media

LinkedIn

https://www.linkedin.com/in/bobpaff

Facebook Business

https://www.facebook.com/CommunicatingToWinLLC

Facebook

https://www.facebook.com/bobpaff

Twitter

https://twitter.com/bobpaff

YouTube

https://www.youtube.com/user/bobpaff

Made in the USA
Middletown, DE
01 June 2015